BUILDING YOUR FUTURE AS
YOUNG AFRICANS

A SUCCESS AND NATION BUILDING COURSE HANDBOOK

Dipo Toby Alakija

CALVARY ROCK
Resources

ISBN: 978-978-3770-515
978-377-051-9

Published In 2017 By
CALVARY ROCK PUBLISHING

19, Ajina Street, Ikenne Remo,
Ogun State, Nigeria.

www.calvaryrock.org

For Christian Education And Ministration Services

INTRODUCTION

I wish to use two events in my country, Nigeria which is in West Africa, to introduce to you this course which centres on orientations of Young African, especially youths.

The first story is about two Secondary School girls who left one town to another with one of their friends to meet a witch doctor in a thickly bushy and lonely area. They chattered a taxi that took them to the place. On getting to the place, the taxi driver was instructed to wait in the cab while the three girls, including their friend went into the bush. When they returned, only the two girls joined the driver. When he asked about the third girl, he was told she would meet them later. As they were driving back, the driver observed them counting huge sum of money through the rear mirror. Then he suspected a foul play. Without giving them room to suspect what he was about to do, he drove them straight to the Police. Investigation revealed that the two girls sold their friend to a witch doctor for rituals. Of course, the poor girl had been dismembered before the arrival of the police.

This story proves that if Secondary School girls could get the nerves to sell their friend for money, Nigeria is in for a very big trouble unless drastic action is taken to forestall the insanity in the society.

The second story is about a friend of mine who is a civil engineer. We worked as children teachers in a Church here in Nigeria some years ago on voluntary basis, using my story books to build the children. He later travelled to London with high expectation. With his impressive qualifications and wealth of experience in civil engineering, he was expected to get a job without any problem. He was soon disillusioned when he could not find a job. Not willing to be an idle person, he went to a Church, gathered the children who normally roamed around, disrupting the service on Sundays. He began to teach them the word of God; using some stories as part of his tools to arrest their attentions. Before anyone knew it, his little children Church had attracted all the young ones that normally roamed about the main Church. When it was discovered that this friend of mine has the skill to handle children, he was employed instantly to work on Sundays as children teacher. If you think that is the end of the story, you are wrong. The children who learnt so much from my friend

1

were fond of telling their parents about him. Most of them wanted them to invite him for dinner. Through that, he got to know a lot of people. Some of them later helped him to set up an engineering company all because he has positively influenced their children. He soon began to earn so much money - much more than what he expected from the job he tried to get.

In the second story, you will observe that there is success in everything a man does, especially the ones that are done in the name of the Lord or humanity. In other words, there is success within each one of us. Preoccupation is what takes our minds away from the enormous opportunities available to us. While many people see problems, very few see the solution to the problem as an opportunity to succeed. My friend did not know that the problem the children constituted in the Church was an opportunity to establish an engineering company. You can never know where the opportunity to solve a problem will take you to. John Lubbock said, *"What we see depends mainly on what we look for."* How true. If all you can see in your environment is problem, it means therefore that all you are looking for is problem and all you will see is problem, not solution.

WHAT MAKES SUCCESS IN LIFE?
What makes success is the question everybody must ask himself. Is it money? Is it level of education? Is it connection? Is it fame? Is it marriage? To get the answer, we must define success.

WHAT IS SUCCESS?
Contrary to what people think, success is not being wealthy or famous or in what you have achieved but rather in living a purposeful and fulfilled life. It is not limited to one area of life. A man may be successful as a businessperson and still be a failure as a married man. He may not be successful in acquiring wealth and yet a great success in other things like in the case of Florence Nightingale who came from a very rich family but sacrificed so much to serve humanity through nursing. Millionaire John Rockefeller admitted, *"I have made millions, but they have brought me no happiness."* The Bible says in Proverb 13:19, *"The desire accomplished is sweet to the soul...."* Success therefore depends on what you want to

2

achieve with your life, how you go about it, the fulfilment of and in the achievement. Success also implies visions and their implementations. These are what can make a person feel fulfilled.

Following this definition, we shall categorize what makes a success into two. They are goals that may be called visions and their implementations. These two will be studied in building your future as a young African.

It is instructive to first note that African youths must not accept the pitiable condition in their countries as their destinies. Some people caused all the problems they are facing now long before most of them were born. The problems will continue to give birth to more and more problems unless citizens change the conditions in these countries by changing their unpatriotic attitudes. What you can change, therefore, is not what you can call a destiny. To prove this point, if Americans are brought to Nigeria while Nigerians are taken to America, in no time, Americans will change Nigeria into America while Nigerians will change America into Nigeria.

GOALS

Zig Ziglar said in his book titled steps to the top, *"The poorest of all men is the one without a dream."* When you look at all the inventions we enjoy today, you will discover that they were once dreams of some people. A lot of people are miserable today because they do not have a dream that will make them lively. Such people may be wealthy or even famous yet they feel very miserable in life. One of the things that can bring life into you is a dream - a vision and expectation. This is what I refer to as a goal in life. The goals you have set for yourself will engage your mind in certain activities which will make you lively and healthy mentally. Science proved that a lot of things depend on your brain, including the working condition of your body. Your mental alertness can help your body recover quickly if you fall sick. Similarly, the hopelessness of a person can bring about frustration and depression which can lead to mental sickness and death. It is therefore important that you set goals for yourself and be prepared to do something good with your life.

There are a number of characteristics in a goal. They are:

3

Measurable, Achievable, Communicable, Tangible and Definitive. Before we talk on each of them, you must understand that there are two types of goals. They are long term and short term goals. The long term goals are what will take years to accomplish such as building a family or a career or a business or having branches of your organization in many areas etc. The short term goals are the ones you have immediate plan to execute such as organizing programme or getting money for house rent or going for a short course. The major focus is on the long term goals that will determine where you will be in future and how you can move forward. In whichever of the two types, you must give yourself good reasons you want to carry out the goals.

Measurable: This aspect of a goal can be defined as a projection or calculating what it takes to achieve the desired result. This is where planning comes in although we shall still discuss that under implementations. When planning, you may or you may not foresee most of the obstacles or problems but definitely, if your goal is measurable, you can see what you want to achieve. John Foster Dulles said, *"the measure of success is not whether you have a tough problem to deal with, but whether it is the same problem you had last year."* The problem you face or foresee is not what makes your goal measurable or not but rather the ability to see from where you are the possibility of achieving the desired result in spite of the problem.

Achievable: When you want to set a goal, you must be realistic and be conscious of your limit. For instance, someone with physical impairment should not think of becoming a football star. Most things that people think cannot be achieved can be achieved. All it takes is faith, mental and physical work. The Bible defines faith in Hebrew 11:1 as the substance of things hope for, the evidence of things not seen. The most difficult and delicate part of any work is the mental work because so much depends on it. The ability to foresee or project the execution of a vision which seems unrealistic distinguishes a man with a vision from others. John Johnson said, *"Men and women are limited not by the place of their birth, not by colour of their skin, but by size of their hope."* If you really put all you can to build a castle in the air, you will end up building a mansion in a beautiful

4

city. If your goal is to be achieved, you must have what it takes to achieve it. You need the courage and determination, the attributes of mental work to achieve your goal. If you are afraid to face a cat, do not dare the lion. If David in the Bible had dreaded the bear and the lion that threatened his father's sheep, he would not have had the courage to face Goliath. Often times, people think they have set achievable goals but in fact they have not. Any achievable goal must be in proportion with your faith and what you are ready to offer or sacrifice to achieve it.

<u>Communicable</u>: Most goals if not all need the support of other people before they can be achieved. It therefore follows that you must be able to carry people along with you in your goals. This is especially true with team and other leaders or those who need the co-operations of other people. Since people are involved in most visions, there is need to communicate them to others before you can carry them along. John C. Maxwell in his book titled "The 21st Indispensable Qualities Of A Leader" gave four basic truths to follow to be effective communicator. They are: Simplify your message, Focus on the person whom you are communicating, Show the truth by believing in what you say and lastly seek response. A vision or goal must be communicable.

<u>Tangible</u>: Tangible in this regard means to be realistic, not imaginary. I have had to counsel a lot of youths who mentioned the people they loved to emulate. Some want to be football stars, while some would like to be music legends and others like that. This can be daydream if they do not put what it takes to be so successful. What most youths do not understand is that people do not become successful by chance or through little efforts. Life is a matter of give and take what you can. Before you get anything from anything you must have given something in kind or cash. In most endeavours, you must give until you begin to get. A farmer who has his hands full of seeds must give some or all of the seeds before he can reap the harvest. If he puts nothing into the ground, he gets nothing. It is good to dream of greatness but there is a price to be paid. Clarence Munn says, *"the difference between great and good is a little extra efforts."* For your vision to be tangible, it must be something you can work

hard for. You can't just stand by and fold your hands, expecting luck to do things for you. Those who do nothing and expect something will have and become nothing as times goes on. The difference between tangible and unrealistic goals is the person that makes it real. Dr. J. A. Holmes said, *'never tell a young person that something cannot be done. God may have been waiting for centuries for somebody ignorant enough of the impossible to do that very thing.'* To illustrate this, I would relate the case of my brother-in-law called T. J Dosumu. He went to a very primitive school in the early eighties in a village in Nigeria where he had his primary and secondary school education. His school certificate result in art subjects was very poor. He started working as a messenger in a Federal Government establishment in Nigeria. When he was working, he had a goal to become a Chemical Engineer. That seemed unrealistic for someone who not only lack science background but also have a lot of obstacles to overcome. But he had one great advantage - a very strong desire to become a Chemical Engineer and faith in God. He worked very hard, communicating his goals to people including a deaf scientist who not only believed he could make it but also took time to teach him science subjects. He took another examination in science subjects and passed. Today, he holds two B.Sc. degrees in Bio-Chemistry (first class, University of Lagos) and Chemical Engineering (second class upper). He achieved his goal and rouse from the post of a messenger to the position of Standard Engineer Officer in the same establishment.

Definitive: This simply means conclusive. Once a goal is set, there should be no going back. It takes determination to carry out goals because you will find every reason to change your mind. There are many things that prevent people from reaching their goals. Some of them include: (i) Fear of the unknown (ii) Indiscipline (iii) Indecision (iv) Fear of what people would say or think and (V) Fear of failure.

When your goal is definitive, you need to begin to take steps and use the resources within your disposal to carry it out. The truth is: no one can use all the abundant resources God had made available to him before he achieves a success. That is why the saying goes: *'when there is life, there is hope.'* Zig A Civil Unrest That Leads To Threats Of Lives And Properties

6

Ziglar said, *'expect the best. Prepare for the worst. Take what comes.'* If you do not take definitive step forward by doing all you can to achieve your goal, you will become stagnant water that offers nothing but stinks and dirty things. As stagnant water harbours and breeds all forms of disgusting objects that range from dead reptiles to fungus plants, so will the person that is not definitive in his goals harbour nothing good except excuses, complaint, criticism, animosity and even jealousy. Such person would learn to laugh at others when they are struggling to achieve their goals and becomes very jealous when they become successful. He will become an impediment to others and later a dependent on the success of others. This is the time to make up your mind to be definitive in your goals.

The above are the characteristics of reasonable goals. We shall discuss implementation as in relation to building your future and the nation now.

IMPLEMENTATION OF GOALS

This is going to be our major focus. It is observed that most people have dreams or desires which I generally described as goals in life but they give up at the implementation stage. They settle for something far below their dreams and live in the dreams of other people who are strong enough to implement their goals in life. Your goal in life is very important to you and many others who would live after you. So your family, community, country and the world cannot afford to let your dreams die for whatever reason. If you let it die, you may deny some people, including your future children some good things. I want you to see this world as a giant pot where people live and contribute their ideas that make life better for others. Such ideas may be in form of inventions, business, education, politics, research works, medicines, entertainments, sports, inspiring books and so many other things. The ideas live on long after the owners have died. Do not think of coming into this world just to enjoy the ideas of others. Let others also enjoy your idea too. It is very important to make your life a success.

At this stage of this study, you need to start thinking of what you want to achieve with your life. If you do not have an idea yet, you do not have to worry about that. You can always read the book over again until you get one. Let us assume you have a goal and then think of its implementation.

We are going to discuss a few things in this aspect of implementation. These are: (i) Action plan (ii) Faith (iii) Preparation (iv) Opportunities.

ACTION PLAN

Someone said that failure to plan is a sure way to fail. Things do not happen by chance. To build a house, you need a plan. To establish any business, you need a plan called feasibility report. Also to live any successful life, you need to plan for that life. You must plan the way you spend your time and money. Before you can implement your goal, you must plan. It is better to take years to plan what will take few weeks to achieve than to spend years trying anything without a plan. In the cause of planning, you may foresee some obstacles and find ways to overcome them. Note here that money is hardly the problem in implementations of goals or visions of a person but the attitude towards it. Remember the old sayings: once there is a will, there is a way. Big goals do not start big. They start very small with the little a person has. Nobody climbs the ladder from the top. You start from the first step, which is having good goals . I know a woman who is now a big time business woman. She started it by selling few cups of salt. In most cases, businesses and endeavours grow as person with the vision grows in experience. When making action plan, be objective in your planning. Let your plan be in proportion with your desire to achieve your goal. To illustrate this, I would share with you the story of one of my classmates in Junior Secondary School. This boy was the dullest student in class. When a student told another student, 'you are as dull as Victor,' (not real name) the student would get real mad. Victor could not go beyond Junior Secondary School level before he changed his plan from education to tailoring. He pursued the plan with passion. He had became successful as a tailor with people working under him before any of us graduated from the University. There was hardly any of the so-called-brilliant students with the assurance of getting jobs after they graduated from schools. Education is very good, believe me, but if you do not have the strong desire that will see you all through, you better focus on something else. After all, if you can read and write, you can get informal education

8

by reading on your own. One wonderful thing about reading is that you can become anything by reading. One of my course mates who lost his mother when he was a child became a College lecturer without going to secondary school. There was no magic about it. He simply had the desire to become a graduate and he became one because he never gave up making personal efforts. When making action plan to implement your goals, you must put the followings into considerations: (i) Is the goal short or long term? (ii) What does it take to implement the goal? (iii) What are my limitations and how do I overcome them? (iv) What are the possible obstacles? (v) Who and what do I need to reach my goals in spite of the obstacles?

Once you are able to answer the above questions reasonably, you are already getting a blueprint of what you need to reach your goal. Note the word "reasonably." You do not need absolute answers to them before you can have a blueprint of your goal. All you need is just the possibility or chances of implementing the goal.

FAITH

Faith has to do with what and whom you believe. Your faith matters a lot in whatever you do in life. Your faith will drive you to do so many things. You can describe faith as convictions or belief. Your faith must be in three things. They are: (i) Faith In God (ii)Faith In Yourself (iii) Faith In Your Goals.

Faith In God: The Bible says in Hebrew 11:6, *'But without faith it is impossible to please him for he that cometh to God must believe that he is, and that he is the rewarder of them that diligently seek him.'* Faith in God makes a person conscious of the fact that He is everywhere. He is all powerful and all knowing. Faith in God moulds character, builds integrity and good relationship with others. Such faith makes a person to fear God. In the Book of Psalms 111:10, the Bible says, *'The fear of the Lord is the beginning of wisdom: a good understanding have all they that do his commandments...'* The fear of God not only make a person wise but also godly. Your character and integrity matters in whatever you want to achieve in life. These are the ways to begin to build faith in God:

(i) Faith in God first comes through reading and hearing the word of God, according to Romans 10:17 in the Bible.

(ii) It grows by living by the word of God, according to what Jesus said in Luke 4:4.

(iii) Read books that will teach you more about God, not cult or other books that will lure you into violence or ungodly acts.

(iv) You need to move with godly people that will positively influence your life and avoid associating with ungodly people (Psalms 1:1-6). You can make friends with people who will help you fuel the fire of your faith, not the ones that will quench it.

Faith In Yourself: Ralph Waldo Emerson said, *"believe in yourself, and what others think won't matter."* Having faith in yourself does not mean you will not make mistakes but, irrespective of that, you need to believe in yourself that you can achieve what you want if you put all you can to get success. A lot of people fail because they lack confidence in themselves. They assume that they cannot achieve a thing without another person. They probably do not appreciate what the Bible says in Psalms 139:14 which states the fact that each person is fearfully and wonderfully made. In other words, each person in this world is a masterpiece of God. This can be proved from the fact that no one - dead or alive have the same fingerprints with another person. So there is no one of the type of anyone. Consequently, each has a gift and a mission peculiar to him. No one, therefore, must feel inferior or superior to another person, no matter highly gifted or intelligent or educated. If you allow any trace of inferiority complex inside you, it is going to affect everything about you. One of the ways this is going to affect you is that the opinions of other people can make you surrender your vision to them. Because you feel inferior to them, you will feel their opinions are superior to yours. If you have a worthy vision, you must have confidence in it, even if it looks so hard to accomplish. I use to tell people who are full of themselves that even if they are more intelligent or professional than me in what I desire to achieve, they cannot be more foolish. You may ask why taking pride in foolishness. My reason is found in 1 Corinthians 4:10 which says, *'We are fools for Christ's sake, but you are wise...'* So whatever a man is made up of, even if people consider it foolishness, it is to the glory of God as long as he is in Christ. I cannot help but to share with you the story of a man who displayed the above passage by writing it in front of his T shirt "I AM A FOOL" and added in much smaller letters, "for Christ's sake." People saw the big letters and started laughing at him. When he walked passed them, they discovered that he had a question for them at the back of the T shirt: "WHOSE FOOL ARE YOU?" That silenced those who were laughing at him. That indicates that no matter how wise a person may be, he is still a fool for something. So foolishness for the sake of Christ looks to me as a virtue we must covet. At least, we all know that God uses foolish things to confound the wise. Ordinarily, it was foolish of David to think of defeating Goliath who had been a warrior since he was young with a stone and a sling but God used that foolishness to give him victory. It was also foolish of Moses to think a way could be made for the people of Israel to pass on the sea with his rod but it worked out. What lies behind what looks like foolishness is the power of God.

When you are conscious of the fact that you are masterpiece of God in His creation, you will have faith in yourself and in your ability. You will not underrate yourself for any reason. Everybody is born with at least an ability. You must not feel inferior to the person with ten talents because you have only one. If you believe so much in that one and work so hard to use It, you can excel more than the person with ten. I was directing a movie some years ago where we could not get enough casts. Some of the ones we had were acting for the first time. There was a lady who could have performed better than any of the new casts but for her feelings of inadequacy and lack of confidence in her ability. Having identified her problem, I told her to act herself if at all she could not pretend to be someone else. Fortunately, she was acting like someone preaching to a sinner. She really performed very well at the end.

Lack of confidence in yourself can affect your performance. So learn to build faith in yourself. Even if you are not yet good enough, keep telling yourself that you are going to do better. Do not listen to those who are looking for area of your weakness instead of strengths. Many critics, especially destructive type will never tell you that, with time and practice, you can improve on your skill even if they know you can. When you are attacked with criticism which you are going to face whether you like it or not, remember what Dale Carnegie said, *"any fool can criticize, condemn, and complain and most fools do."* You must understand that you know something which critics do not know. So if there is anyone that will have more faith in you, it is you, yourself; not critics or friends or even family. Some people may have faith in you and what you can do with your potentials but if you do not have faith in yourself, it will amount to nothing. You must have faith that you have all it takes to carry out your goals in life, irrespective of what others think or say.

The followings are the ways you can start building faith in yourself:

(i) Engage yourself in the work that is relevant to your interest or gifts. Be involved in church activities, social or community works. If you cannot get someone to engage you, form a club that will engage and serve people for free. My engineer friend did not know that God was preparing him for the work in the Church that would pay him in London when he was teaching children in the Church in Nigeria. As you engage yourself in what seems minor, you will be building the skill and faith in yourself.

(ii) Spend quality time to study and share what you have learned with other people. This can help you to overcome certain weakness which you may not be aware of. Apart from that, you will begin to gain confidence in your communication skill which is vital if you really want to communicate or share your vision with others.

(iii) Identify the area of your weakness that poses threats to your goal and discipline yourself to overcome it. If you eat too much, put yourself into fasting. If you are extravagant, cut down your expenses. If you sleep too much, cultivate the habit of walking round the room while you read. If you are always afraid, always face the thing you fear so much. As you grow over your weakness, you will begin to build more confidence in yourself. Gilbert Arland said, *"when an archer misses the mark he turns and looks for fault within himself. Failure to hit the bull's-eye is never the fault of the target. To improve your aim, improve yourself."*

(iv) Always take up the challenges people always shy away from even if you know the price is great. That is what would make you outstanding and full of faith. Consider the common characteristics in the people that strive for excellence in the second book of Timothy 2:3-6 in the Bible. The people are considered soldiers in verse 4, athletes in verse 5 and farmers in verse 6. The three of them have the followings in common: (a) discipline (b) endurance (c) determination (d) readiness to face challenges and (e) hope to get desired result. These must be present in anyone who desire any success in life. After all, life is a challenge. So take up the challenge which others shy away from.

Faith In Your Vision Or Goal: To have faith in any goal, you must have a goal which must have the characteristics which had been explained earlier. It is not enough to have a goal that is measurable, achievable, communicable, tangible and definitive. You must have faith in the goal. John C. Maxwell said, *"a difficult crisis can be more readily endured if we retain the conviction that our existence holds a purpose, a cause to pursue, a person to love, a goal to achieve."* There are some factors that determine the growth of faith in your goal. But first, it is instructive to note that the faith you have in your goal will determine how far you can go in the midst of oppositions. Every good goal always face oppositions, some of which are fierce enough to make you give it up. The good news is: you can achieve what you want to achieve. Theodore Epp says, *"our strength is seen in the things we stand for; our weakness is seen in the things we fall for."* If you fall for the opposition to give up your goal, you are weak and you are not worthy of that goal. The Bible says in Proverbs 24:10, *'If you faint in the day of adversity, your strength is small.'* If you really have a goal in life, your faith in it will sustain you in the days you are forced to give it up. It may be mere criticism that will try to lay you off your plan. David Brinkley said, *"a successful man is one who can lay a firm foundation with bricks others have thrown at him."* The bad news about giving up your goal is that you will find it more difficult to achieve another good goal, no matter how promising it may be. But if you press on in your goal, you will find enough strength to continue as you hang on. When you succeed in carrying out your goal, you will have more strength and confidence to go for greater goal like Alexander, the great who got more and more powerful as he conquered one empire after the other until there was no more empire for him to conquer. If you do not have faith in your goal, do not attempt to achieve it because you will be forced to give it up when it is tried. John C Maxwell said, *'if your vision doesn't cost you anything, it is daydream.'* Only your faith in it will make it stand. Henry James makes us to understand that until we try, we don't know what we can't do. Zig Ziglar encouraged, *'keep trying. It is only from the valley that the mountain seems high.'* In other words, the height of your goal does not matter. It is the height of your faith in it that matters. You may set a small goal and still fail if you don't have enough faith in it to make it succeed. The factors responsible for growth of faith in a goal are as follows:

(i) What you know about your vison or goal will determine your faith in it. The more you learn about it, the more you know that it can be achieved.

(ii) The people you associate with are another good factor that can make your faith to grow or die. Do you associate with people who have no goals for their lives? Mark Twain said, *"Keep away from people who belittle your ambition. Small people always do that but the really great people make you feel that you, too, can become great."* Small people naturally want to make others feel smaller while real great people will make them to feel they can be greater. If you are always in the company of those who will encourage you, your faith in your goal in life will increase. Share your goals in life only with those who will encourage you, not those who will discourage you or kill it with pessimism. The Bible says in Philippians 3: 2, *'Beware of dogs, beware of evil workers, beware of the concision.'*

(iii) The time you spend, planning and thinking of your goal in life will help your faith in it to grow. When you spend more time, planning and thinking about your goals, you will foresee hindrances and ways to overcome them. Again, you must know that there is nothing like hassle free goal in life. Everything a man wants to achieve in life has some elements of difficulties and even risks built inside it.

(iv) Take some steps towards your goal, no matter how

14

minor it seems. The steps you have taken so far to achieve your goal will increase your faith in it. If you can, create an environment that will make it very difficult for you to give it up. For instance, when I was working as a civil servant, I had the vision to become an international writer, publisher, a resource person and film producer who would make impact in the lives of all categories of people including children. It was a good job because I was well paid but it was a serious hindrance for me to carry out these goal. I had a lot of people depending on my salary but I knew I had to resign my appointment with the Federal Government in Nigeria if I must carry out my visions. Considering the size of the economic problem in the country back then, it would be foolish, if not crazy to resign. I became very unpopular in my family when I left the job. I no longer had any source of income. So I had no choice but to struggle hard to carry out the vision, at least to prove it to people that I knew what I was doing. It took me time but I began to reach my goal. In 2001, I managed to publish my first book which is not really a book but a pamphlet. It was so appreciated that it was sold in several thousands of copies. The proceed was used to establish a school for my wife. The success of one goal gave room for others to succeed. Today, by the Grace of God I have written and published many books that are used to make impact in different parts of the world, including Europe and US. I have produced a number of films including "The Black Worshippers" which was used to fight cultism in so many secondary schools and tertiary institutions in the late 1990s. Besides that, I write for newspapers and feature in television programmes. I am saying this to make an impact in, not to impress you. I am an ordinary person just like everyone. What makes a difference is what I am sharing with you. Vince Lombardi said, *'the harder you work, the harder it is to surrender.'* You must work out your success yourself. Nobody is going to work it out for you. The Bible says in Proverbs 20:4, *'The sluggard will not plow by reason of the cold; therefore shall he beg in the harvest, and have nothing.'* If lazy people do not beg to get food, they will resolve to stealing or getting involved in social vices, making life difficult for other people.

15

PREPARATION

Contrary to general opinion, preparation to achieve a goal is in everyday activities. It is not limited to what you are taught in the school or what you have read in books or in the people you meet everyday. It is also in what you do everyday with what you have learnt. What you do today is your preparation for tomorrow. If you invest your time playing piano, the chances are that you may become a professional pianist. Whatever you spend your time doing is what you will improve upon. There were times in my life when all I was doing was to read and write. You can judge if there is trace of professionalism in my writings. If you spend your time partying or watching movies that have nothing to offer you, you will end up a destitute that depends on others for survival. You must note that there are things people do that rob them of valuable things in future and there are things others do that enhance their value in life. Zig Ziglar said, *"the present day is important to you for this reason: you can waste it or use it, but no matter how you spend it, you've traded a day of your life for it."* Joseph C. Grew has this to say, *"we cannot pause, or hesitate, or kill time as if you could kill time without injuring eternity."* The Bible makes us to understand in Ecclesiastes 3:1-8 that there is a season and a time for everything, including a time to be born and to die. You have the options of spending your time preparing to reach your goal or spend it watching meaningless television programmes or films instead of reading, spend so much time chatting on the internet instead of gathering information that will help you reach your goal. Some spend the whole day with friends who have no focus in life. In anything anyone wants to achieve in life, there is no shortcut. Shortcuts shorten success and sometimes life. A man who steals or robs others only risk going to jail or getting killed also. A man who is dishonest only risks losing his job and his integrity with others, thereby finding it difficult to get an employment or risks not having people doing business with him. A student who cheats during the examination only risks being caught or missing the chance to get assurance that he can defend his certificate when he graduates. There is absolutely no shortcuts to success. Most shortcuts lead to failures, destruction of potentials or loss of lives.

When preparing to reach your goal, you must work on the followings: (i) Your Attitude (ii) Your Skill and (iii) Available Resources.

We shall treat each as they relate to preparation for your success. Before then, it is instructive to note that preparation is the first thing you need to make before you can make best use of the opportunity to reach your goal. As Myles Munroe said, success comes when preparation meets with opportunities. Of all the two, you can only control one and that is preparation.

Your attitude: Your attitude is your greatest asset or major obstacle to achieve your goal in life. Attitude is the starting point of any success be it in life, marriage, business - any mission in life. Your attitude has a lot to do with the way you think, how you feel or react to any situation. It also has to do with what you say and do. If what you say match what you do, you will build the integrity that will help you reach your goal. If they do not match, you will be seen as inconsistent or even dishonest. In business, honesty is regarded as the best policy anywhere. The attributes that are stated in 2 Peter 1:5-8 are essentials for a person to be successful and prosperous. These attributes includes diligence, faith, virtues, knowledge, temperance, patience, brotherly kindness and charity. All these are considered godliness.

There is need for people who want to be successful in life to abide by the following Biblical principles :

(i) They must first seek the kingdom of God and His righteousness, according to Matthew 6:33.
(ii) They must obey the Word of God. That is the condition attached to the blessings in Deuteronomy 28: 1-13.
(iii) They need to allow others to benefit from your blessings according to Luke 12:33.

For you to prepare to achieve your goal, you must do all you can to improve on your attitude. Everybody needs positive attitude towards everything in life, towards his enemies and in stormy situations. Kenneth Copeland said, 'your gift will take you places but your character will keep you there.' Since people are the reflection of what a person is in the inside, he will seem surrounded by nice people if he is nice to them. Anyone with problem of attitude will seem surrounded by mean people. I know a man who despite the fact that he was not rich made people happy. He loved to visit people in their homes so as to know how to pray and meet their needs. Somehow through prayers and personal commitments, he always found solutions to their problems. This man fell sick one day. He was in dire need of blood before he could survive. News about his condition spread round the town. Guess what. The whole town stormed the hospital, ready to drain their blood for that man. If there is anything we must improve on in our lives it is our attitudes. Real great people through selfless service and positive attitudes serve as role models to others. Do all you can to improve on your attitude through selfless services and support of others instead of thinking of yourself alone. Edward Bulwer Lytton said, *"a good heart is better than all the heads in the world."* I remember a teacher who mercilessly beat a boy in his class to the extent that he sustained a permanent bump on the forehead for a trivial offence. Even though the teacher was unrepentant but because the parents are Christians, they not only forgave him but also taught the boy to forgive him. Years later, the boy became a lecturer in a university at the time the teacher was just going for a degree course in the same institution. The lecturer recognized him and went to identify himself to the teacher. The teacher began to apologize for his negative attitude many years before. We all have a chance to show a little kindness to our follow human beings. You can never tell what it means to your success in life or what it will fetch you in future. I cannot help but to share with you the story of a man who struggled to take care of the twin brothers in Nigeria. The brothers later travelled to the United States. After some years, they came for a visit in Nigeria and decided to see the man that took care of them. They found him in the same condition they had left him. These twin brothers helped the man to get to the United States where he became a successful person. You have probably heard that both good and evil have their rewards. The one you are involved in will determine where you will end up. Robespierre said, *"no man can climb out beyond the limitations of his own character."*

Your Skill: This is what makes you a valuable asset to yourself, your family, country and the world. What you know add value to you. For instance this book you are reading is not worth spending your time reading if it is blank paper. But value had been added to it by the teachings. The teachings won't be worth studying if they are not written with skill. The same thing with an individual. The greatest asset in a country is the number of active and skillful people in the nation, not the amount of wealth inside it. People who do not contribute their manpower resources into the economy eat out the reserve of the nation. So no matter how rich a country may be in natural resources, if there are no hands to add value to what is on ground, the people will sooner or later become poor in the midst of plenty. That is why many countries in Africa are still poor in the midst of plenty. Those who are supposed to be acquiring skills in schools or other places are already nursing babies that would later depend on others for survival. The number of beggars and touts in the streets in many african countries is staggering. So many children who are supposed to be in schools are asking for alms everyday. Many people in these countries depend so much on the government to give them everything they need. Government should not only get them employment but also provide the food and cook it for them. People who expect so much from their governments without making efforts to help themselves become frustrated. When they get frustrated, they turn to robbery or prostitution or other anti-social activities. What baffles me most in people is the amount of skills that are not used. Plutarch said, *'the richest soil, uncultivated produces the rankest weeds.'* Many African nations are rich in everything - natural and human resources but they are full of thick weeds because they are not cultivated. Who is to cultivate them? The citizens who reside in each of these countries. Since there is no free lunch anywhere, not even in Freetown in Sierra Leone, and since life is give and take, each person must give in kind, goods or service before he can get something in return. God will never bless idle hand. When God created Adam and Eve, he told them to till the ground. J. G. Holland said, *'God gives every bird its food, but He does not throw it into the nest.'* You can see why you have to add value to yourself by acquiring skills before you can make success in your endeavours. You need to work towards your vision or goal by developing the skill you need.

These are the ways to develop your skill:

(a) You must constantly practice what you want to develop within you. Macauley said, *"just remember that if you are not working at your game to the utmost of your ability, there will be someone out there somewhere with equal ability. And one day, you'll play each other, and he'll have the advantage."*

(b) You must learn from other people who are skillful in the area of your goal and also learn from your mistakes and mistakes of others.

(c) Ask questions, no matter how foolish they sound. An inquisitive mind always enrich the head with knowledge. If you do not understand what you are being taught in the school, do not be too shy or proud to ask questions. If you do not ask questions about what you don't know, you will miss the opportunity to add more to your knowledge. After all, no one can claim to be an island of knowledge. I remember asking my biology class teacher when he was teaching us about insects in Junior Secondary School. I said almost foolishly, "sir, can you explain why God created flies, since it has nothing good to offer except diseases?" That question sounded so funny that everybody including the teacher laughed. The teacher made me realized that it was an intelligent question because he could see that I wanted to know about life circle which was meant for the higher class. He repeated the question in other classes and among the teachers. I became a star in that school for asking question that almost sounded so foolish. I also asked a lot of questions from the person that taught me some techniques in film production.

(d) You must cultivate the habit of reading books related to your career, not just any book. Through that you can learn from others. I read some of the books that are used to train teachers by National Teachers' institute, Kaduna in Nigeria because I want to develop the skill in teaching young ones and in writing for them. They are not small books. So it was like I was going on course without an instructor but the knowledge I acquired from the books justify my efforts. Although I do not possess the certificates of a professional children teacher but I can teach just like any good teacher and also write like any other good children book writer. In fact, the book titled "The Young Generation Story Book" and other children book are used by lots of professional teachers to teach children in primary schools and Churches. I did not get the skill by chance. Nothing like skills come by chance. Even if a person is gifted, he would still need to develop that gift. I learned from professionals through their books. The skills are all there for everyone to acquire. You have to discipline yourself enough to acquire it. Skill is what makes a difference between a professional or a skilled person and the unskilled labourer just as ability to work distinguishes a worker from a destitute who has nothing to offer in terms of service. It is also a pity that many people think of certificate alone instead of focusing on skill acquisitions. Skills are like images while certificates are the shadows of the images. A shadow can do nothing of its own while images can. Because most of the systems in Africa are designed to celebrate graduates with or without skills, most youths of nowadays are chasing the shadows instead of the images. For this reason, there are many jobless graduates who look up to the Government to offer them jobs. If you can get the image (skills) of your own, you will get employed or create jobs that will control by engaging the shadows (others) that have no images.

(e) You must have the strong desire to acquire the skill. Your desire will cause you to explore every chance to develop the skill you need before you can reach your goal. John C Maxwell said, *"if you follow your passion - instead of other's perceptions - you can't help becoming a more dedicated, productive person."*

RESOURCES

Resources can be simply divided into three categories, known as the three big Ms. They are (1) Money (2) Materials and (3) Manpower.

We are going to discuss each as they are related to building your future as a young African.

MONEY: Money had always been a source of great controversy all over the world from time immemorial. The Bible says in 1 Timothy 6: 10, *'For the love of money is the root of all evil: which while some coveted after, they have erred from faith, and pierced themselves with many sorrows.'* Money can be a good source of evil, problems and sorrow according to that passage and yet we all need money. Every organization, business or individual needs money to operate successfully. Without money one can hardly achieve anything. Money is used in business, it is used to pay salaries of workers, it is used to pay school fees, it is used to meet personal needs, to maintain ourselves and to do all sorts of things that relate to life and everyday activities. The question now is: How can a person make legitimate money without having to do evil or rob others or the nation? The following principles are basic, broad and general ways.

(a) First of all, you need a vision or a marketable idea or service you want to render to the people. This vision will involve meeting people's need since you are going to make money through them. A lot of people think they need money first before they can execute an idea or project. It is not necessarily so. What a person needs for a start is the idea or knowledge of what he wants to do. As pointed out earlier, there is no free lunch anywhere. You cannot touch people's pockets without meeting their needs or touching their hearts unless you want to steal from them. You probably paid for this book before you got it. If it does not suit what you want, you may not read or buy it. Similarly, if you do not market things or render any service, you would be dependent on others or probably begging for alms.

(b) After getting a vision or a marketable idea, you need to learn or get more information about what you want to do. All business companies you see around you are ideas conceived by individuals through visions. In most cases, you need to connect with people who will help or teach you. There are so many people who are looking for where to invest their money. Just because most or all of the people you meet are not interested in your idea or project does not mean that no one would buy your idea. Visions or business ideas give birth to dreams that can be translated into fulfillment. Any vision or goal without idea of how to translate it into reality is daydream. The adage says that if dreams were horses, beggars will ride. But dreams are not horses. So daydreamers do not have any horse to ride to fulfillment. People who do not make efforts to translate their dreams into fulfilment will live in Fools' Paradise. Even

22

if you believe God will to help you carry out your vision, you still need to make lots of efforts to carry out your idea. The Bible confirms this in James 2:26 *"For as the body without the spirit is dead, so faith without works is dead also."*

(c) If you have the money to spend on your idea, why not spend it? If not, the idea will die a natural death. You have probably heard the adage that says: *nothing ventured, nothing gained.* The risk a man refused to take in carrying out his vision will affect him in his progress. A visionary person is always prepared to take calculated financial risks.

When I was going into publishing business, I have to save some money that was very hard to get at that time. I published the first edition of Calvary Rock Periodical in 1995 in Nigeria, hoping to get more money when it was launched. It was a flop. Back then, it was so expensive to publish magazines that I had to save some money the following year before I could afford to publish another edition. Again, it was a flop. The printer's devil came with his ugly performance and messed up the whole publication. In the process of all these, I was learning vital lessons; knowing fully well that the income of each year of my life is going into the publication. I waited again for another year to gather some money and put it into the publication. At last, I got the result I wanted. In fact, that edition launched me into film production in 1997. If you believe in your vision, you will invest in it and if you want to make money, you must spend money.

(d) You need to be meticulous and very prudent in the way you spend your money. A good business man knows that if he wants to have more money, he must increase his income and cut down his expenses wherever possible. For this reason, companies are aggressive in marketing their products or services. Every amount of money a person wastes will affect him or her sooner or later. No one can, therefore, afford to waste money.

Africa is blessed with many things, including manpower and natural resources which secure financial resources for the continent. This makes one to wonder why there is so much poverty which gives birth to all sorts of crimes and terrorism. There are corruptions, dishonesty and fraudulent practice in most African countries. The civil servants are involved in corruptions for whatever reason. Children and youths who watch their parents at home, teachers in schools and political leaders making money in such dirty ways often become threats to the nation years later. The young ones who look for money by all means instead of staying in schools and enhance their values are supposed to be the major concern of every nation in Africa.

These social and economic problems often times make many youths to get involved in prostitution, fraudulent practice, pickpocketing, armed robberies, blood money (killing people for money), ritual killings like the two secondary school girls who sold their friend to a witch doctor in Nigeria. The atrocities in Africa are endless. However, this is not to make anyone feel hopeless about the situation in Africa but to let you see how much your country and the continent need your help. If you cannot help the continent, do not add to the problems by getting involved in vices or crimes or rebellion against the Government in your country. Do not join any group that will instruct you to take law into your hands. The bad state of the continent is more than enough to affect all the generations yet unborn in Africa without anyone adding to the problems. As a young African, you are the solution to the problems in your country, not part of them. To be the solution, you must first fit into the National Value System by obeying the law, rules and regulations; campaigning against vices and crimes in your country. You also have to understand the need to add value to yourself through the things you are being taught in this book so that you can be reasonable, responsible and productive member of the society. You have to build your country by first building yourself without expecting anyone to come and help you otherwise the generation that is coming behind you would question you of our own efforts to put things right just as everybody is looking for whom to blame. God has given every nation the potentials like the will of people, the financial resources and other means to build and make it pleasant to live. Do not leave your responsibilities to others and do not leave your country because it is in bad shape. If citizens in the country you are going have not built theirs, would you think of going there? All a nation needs to excel is the will of the collective people. Individuals should stop wasting money on anything that does not yield good results. Stop buying what you do not need. Use the money to invest in yourself and in young ones through education and skill acquisitions.

MATERIAL: Contrary to what most people think, material is not limited to physical things like crude oil, gold and other things that can be used to get money, materials can also come in form of ideas. Such materials (in form of ideas) can be translated into finished products (in form of goods and services). The most neglected materials in the whole world today are ideas. In fact all goods and services you see around emerged from ideas. A friend of mine said, *"the most important commodity in the world of business is a marketable idea that is properly implemented and extensively publicized."* You need to come up with ideas. When you have one, you are naturally getting ready to reach your goal. The world is full of material resources which include the ideas inside you and me. A lot of people including the ones with ideas are becoming liabilities to their countries instead of becoming blessings. If everybody is contributing his or her ideas into the numerous physical materials on ground, a lot of problems in Africa will naturally disappear. No matter the physical materials in a country, it would amount to nothing if citizens with ideas do not bring them into use. For instance, the building you reside in would be nothing but sand if there is no idea to assemble the materials together to make it a building. In short, ideas make useless things valuable. Everything a person needs to excel in life is within him and everything a country needs to be prosperous is within the country. There are so many countries that are not as blessed as some African nations in terms of natural and human resources but because the people have ideas, they are by far more prosperous. Why? The solution can be explained under manpower resources. As there are some dangerous materials like toxic wastes, there are some undesirable ideas that can draw the nation backward or destroy its potentials. Such ideas only focus on selfish interests of some people such as ruling the country by force, buying or selling votes, rigging of elections, fraudulent practice, mismanagement and embezzlement of public fund. Those who get involved in these practice do not have the interests of their countries in their minds. If a person rob a nation, the people, including the ones that yet unborn are going to pay for it. The Bible says in Ezekiel 18:2 *"What mean ye, that ye use this proverb concerning the land of Israel, saying, The fathers have eaten sour grapes, and the children's teeth are set on edge?"* The Proverb in this passage which is very applicable in all African countries simply means that the older generation did something wrong but the younger generations are the ones that feel much of the pains.

MANPOWER: It is not possible to treat everything about manpower resources in this teaching. However, we shall treat the primary aspect of it as it relates to building your future as a young African.

Manpower resources has to do with human beings. To begin with, I want to paint the picture of the potentials of human beings in relation to money and material resources through the story of a woman and her children.

It was during the stiff regime of the Military Government in Nigeria in the late 1980s, the time things were very tough for everyone in the country, that this woman lost her husband. The man died of minor ailment which could have been treated if the family could pay afford to pay the medical bill, leaving the woman with three children to cater for.

This woman has two options that were common for survival back then. She either resolved to steal or go into prostitution. The other alternative was to get a job. The last option was nearly impossible because many businesses were folding up. Most of the existing ones were owing their workers several months of salaries. That was the situation the woman found herself. As a Christian, she knew she must not sell herself to the rich men that were ready to take advantage of her condition even though there were three children that were counting on her to survive. The woman made up her mind that she would rather die than to steal or sell herself into prostitution. Because of that firm decision, she found the way out of the problem. She went to those selling bean cakes known in Yoruba Land as "akara". To make the bean cakes, the coats of all the beans would have to be removed and washed away with water before it is grinded and fried. Most of the people who sell this type of food do not know that the

26

coats of the beans are very nutritious. Thus they always threw them away. This woman explained her condition to those selling bean cakes in other to get their co-operation. She would tell them that all she needed as help was for them to reserve for her the coats of the beans instead of throwing them away. She would get the bean coats at times with some beans which the people would deliberately leave for her. She would grind, pack it in tins and cook it in a pot. She not only provided food for herself and her children but also sold some to get money to buy other things they need in the house. As long as there were people that were selling the bean cakes, she would get food to eat. Today, her story has changed. She now lives a much more comfortable life with her children. Someone changed this proverb: "necessity is the mother of invention" into "poverty is the mother of innovation". To some extent, he is right because a man may not make full use of his head if he gets all the comfort he needs. That is why people must see every problem as an opportunity to make best use of their potentials, not as excuses to get involved in vices and crime. This can be done by simply studying the problem and finding ways to solve the one you feel you can solve. The problems of diseases which are expensive to cure in hospitals in some African countries like Nigeria for instance is causing the business of herbal medication to boom, making many people millionaires within few years.

A lot of things depend on manpower resources. It is man that combines resources together and brings good result. If manpower is defective, other resources would be wasted or made useless. If other resources are defective, manpower resource can make them effective. Man creates things with his creative ability by putting together into use the materials which had been provided in abundance by God. God did not create anything again after creating the world and human beings because he had created everything for the world to advance right from the beginning. In other words, everything you see around comes from the ground. It is man that combines the natural things to make all the things we see today. Cars, houses, money, computers name it - were all made from the ground except, of course, if someone wants to point out the one that drops from the sky. Nothing is ever a product of accident as some people think. It takes the creative power of someone to bring them into being. God created man and man created all the things you see around. I expect that to make sense to you. If anyone thinks he can reach his goal in life by accident, he is going to wait until he gets to the grave.

Everybody on earth is born with at least an ability. Thus each has a mission assigned to him by God. There is no way he can know or understand the assignment without knowing God through His Son, Jesus Christ. Although many are able to perceive their missions through their natural gifts but they cannot excel in it as they ought to without knowing God. If anyone does not understand the purpose of his being, two things can happen. He will either use his talent to create limited success for himself with the creative power God has given to everybody or he will use it against others. Even if he creates success through his natural gift, putting God aside, he is not likely going to feel fulfilled in life. That is why many rich people die as sorrowful people. It may surprise you to note that some rich people commit suicides. The cause of that may be attributed to the source of their so-called successes.

There is a real life story of a father who took his son on a trip to the country side with the purpose of showing him how poor people live though he lacked the proper understanding of who is actually poor or rich.

They spent two days and nights on the farm of those who they considered a very poor family. When returning from their trip, the father asked his son, "how was the trip?"

"It was great, Dad."

"Did you see how poor people live?" the father asked.

"Oh yeah," said the son.

"So, tell me, what did you learn from the trip?"

The son replied, "I saw that we have one dog and they had four. We have a pool that reaches to the middle of our garden, and they have a stream that has no end. We have imported lanterns in our garden, and they have the stars at night. Our patio reaches to the front yard and they have the whole horizon. We have a small piece of land to live on, and they have fields that go beyond our sight. We have servants who serve us, but they serve others. We buy our food, but they grow theirs. We have walls around out property to protect us,

28

they have friends to protect them."

The boy's father was speechless. His son added, "Thanks, Dad, for showing me how poor we are."

The point to note here is that: being rich or poor depends on individuals' perceptions. This perception is what makes individual a success or failure, a rich or a poor person. These perceptions influence behaviours of individuals. While responsible people take pride and joy in making money through their sweats, the irresponsible ones look for money at the expense of their peace. When a person does what is expected of him as a responsible citizen, using what he has at his disposal, he will please God, his country, the people and himself also, feeling peaceful; joyous and fulfilled. The followings are what make manpower defective or dangerous or a failure:

(a) <u>Greed or selfishness</u>. The Bible says in Proverbs 3:27-28, *'withhold not good from them whom it is due, when it is in the power of your hand to do it. Say not unto your neighbour, Go, and come again, and tomorrow I will give; when you have it with you.'* Greed or selfishness which is one of the most terrible attitudes in a man is lack of consideration for others. If people are concerned about themselves alone, they can do anything to please themselves, including taking the lives of others. They are often surrounded by people who are equally interested in themselves alone.

Two of the characteristics of great people are selflessness and generosity. Richard Foster advised, *"just the very act of letting go of money, or some treasure, does something within us. It destroys the demon of greed."* John Bunyan has this to say, *"you have not lived today until you have done something for someone who can never repay you."* Great people always prove that they are interested in the success of others by doing all they can to help them to become successful in life.

(b) <u>Pride</u>. This alone can make a person a big failure in life. It can destroy the potentials and also the lives of proud people, according to Proverb 16:18 and 29:23. No one has any reason to be proud because we are all picked from the dust. Sooner or later our bodies will go back to the dust. We did not bring anything into this world and we shall take nothing. A good looking person did not create himself and no one can say someone is too beautiful to be kept in grave when he or she dies. Likewise, a wise person cannot claim he gets his wisdom through his own efforts. So no one has got anything to be proud of. Not only God resents pride but people also dislike proud people. If you want to deal with people, you must be humble because it is humility that makes_people great while pride makes them fall into low class. It is not their status in life that makes them great or not. People in business appreciate the fact that they need to be humble and tolerant in the way they deal with their customers if they want to remain in business and so do anyone who is dealing with human beings.

(c) Laziness: This can make man a complete failure. The Bible says in Proverbs 6:9-11, *'How long will you sleep, O sluggard? When will you arise out of your sleep? Yet a little sleep, a little slumber, a little folding of the hands to sleep: So shall your poverty come upon you like a vagabond, and your want like an armed man.'* A person who cannot work with his hands or brain will end up a destitute. While waiting for God to make way for you in your endeavours or business or career, you must be doing something that will earn you income or that will enhance your skill or value in life. Nothing stops a College graduate from acquiring skills in tailoring or other professions. Conrad Hilton said, *"success seems connected with action. Successful people keep moving. They make mistakes, but they don't quit."*

(D) Ignorance: is another factor that can make a person a failure. The Bible says in Hosea 4:6 that the people of God are destroyed for lack of knowledge. Note the difference between knowledge and wisdom. Knowledge is what a person knows - the information he has. Wisdom is synonymous to intelligence. So it is possible to be wise and not knowledgeable. When a person lack information about a particular thing, he is said to be ignorant of that thing. People go to school, not because they are foolish but because they do not want to be ignorant. When a person is born, he has nothing in his head but brain that can be compared with blank tape. As he grows, he begins to gather information which he will later interpret as he grows up. At the age he is able to comprehend the information, he begins to learn some things. What he learns or develops within himself in his environment would make him either valuable to the people and the country or useless or even at times dangerous to the nation. If he learns the right thing, he would be a blessing to that country but if he learns the wrong thing, he would pose a very serious problem or a threat to many things including lives.

In every given society, community, organization or group; human capital are the most valuable assets. For you to prepare yourself to become a valuable asset to yourself and your country, you must do the followings:

(i) Make proper evaluation of yourself by identifying your talents, gifts, interest, abilities and disabilities. Through that, you can know what you can achieve with your life. You may have ten talents and still think you have just five. You may have the ability to teach and think all you can do is to read. Think of the good things people are saying about your gift but do not mind the cynics who think you cannot achieve a thing. When I was in secondary school, I was so poor in science subjects that I dared not think of becoming a scientist. So I worked hard on art subjects, especially English language and Literature since I planned to become a writer. I write stories and essays and gave them to my friends to read. Their responses really encouraged me. When you identify your abilities and disabilities, you must begin to work on them by putting them into practice and making up for them respectfully.

(ii) Make up your mind never to compromise your faith in God even if others compromise. Take stand against all forms of vices or evils. You will be taking stand with God if you do. I like to quote Edmund Burke all the time. He said, *"the only thing necessary for the triumph of evil is for good men to do nothing."* Let people know what you stand for. If they know this, no one will try to persuade you to commit sin. The Bible says in 1 Thessalonians 5:22, "Abstain from all appearance of evil."

(iii) After you have made up your mind to take stand with God by living a responsible life, you must add value to yourself by acquiring knowledge and skills. You do not need to do a job because of the money you will get from it alone but also to acquire skill. You will need the skill long after you have spent all the money you make from it. Sometimes, it is good to work for free if it will enhance your value or skill. The case of my civil engineer friend in London is a classic example. If you graduate from school, instead of waiting for nothing to happen, take up a teaching job even if they are paying you nothing to write home about. Who knows if that will give you the breakthrough you need like my engineer friend. Unknown to many people, the service they render to others in the name of the Lord always add to their values or skills. I know of so many successful gospel musicians who began their careers as Church choirs. My dormant talent in acting was activated when I was a Children Pastor. The children always forced me to interpret many roles with actions whenever I was telling them stories. They wanted to know how a fish swims. They wanted to hear the dog barking. I remember how I fell down from the table while trying to show the children how a monkey jumped from one tree to another. They laughed at me and asked if that was the way monkey fell from the tree. I replied, 'no! I'm not a monkey. That's why I fell. It's hard for a monkey to fall from the tree.'

OPPORTUNITIES

You have probably heard that opportunity comes once in a while. That may not be true to some extent. The opportunity to excel is always around. The reason most people do not see it is because it is sometimes buried somewhere. It is sometimes flying. You have to search for it as if you are looking for hidden treasures. You can also catch an opportunity as if you are trying to catch a bird. The good news is: it is always around. You will find it if you make efforts to look for it. The bad news is: it will always fly away if you are not prepared to catch it. No matter how much you try, you cannot catch the opportunity if you are not prepared for. That is why I have taken time to take you through the period of preparation. With the advent of technology, opportunities are flying like birds all over the world. You can catch some through the newspapers, the internet, radio, television, in the school, in the street - everywhere. But the problem is many people are not prepared for the opportunities that are flying around. John C Maxwell advised, *"don't wait for opportunity to knock. Opportunity doesn't come to the door knocking. You've got to go out and look for it. Take stock of your assets, talents, and resources. Doing that will give you an idea of your potentials...opportunity is everywhere."* The length of preparation and the amount of value you have added to yourself will determine how you will soar.

Some people are like chicken that see every creeping thing as opportunity to eat, spending the whole day picking the ground. People in this category are common. They do not see beyond their immediate environment. So they see little things like employment or going abroad as golden opportunities to be comfortable. Instead of ploughing for harvest, they pick the ground and settle for something relatively small. If someone in the class of uncommon bird comes with an idea that works, the people in the class of chicken flock to do the same thing as if there is no other idea that can work. They cannot try new ideas, break new ground and try an invention because they are thinking of immediate income. Zig Ziglar said, *"go as far as you can see, and when you get there you will always be able to see further."*

Another class of people we have can be compared with a hawk. These people only see the opportunities to use others to their own advantages. They are not interested in exploring opportunities to excel even though they can see it. They do not have much ideas but they know how to steal other people's ideas. They have good eyes to see far and beyond because of their position in life but they would never use it for the good of others. Instead, they take undue advantage of a lot of chicken, especially the young ones who have no experience of how to protect themselves or their potentials. They use these young ones as political thugs, assassins and armed robbers. Some made prostitutes out of the girls that are young enough to be their grand children while some lure young girls from their parents and use them as sex slaves in other countries. They expose them to the danger of catching Sexually Transmitted Diseases (STD), creating the chances of meeting their untimely deaths. They sometimes use them to push hard drugs and made them to face jail sentence in the country that is far from their homes. I can never exhaust all the atrocities of these hawks but I want to relate the case of a girl who sold her future for temporary pleasure. Her story was published in a Nigerian newspapers some years ago. She had boyfriends, including sugar daddies who met her needs when she was in school. One day, one of her boyfriends took her to a house where there were three other men. She was entertained with some drinks that was mixed with drug. She was not herself after taking the drinks, acting like a wild girl as the three men slept with her. After coming back to her senses, she knew she must not mess around with just any man. She later in the years fell in deep love with a man that was ready to make life very comfortable for her. They soon began to plan for their wedding but somehow, the man's brother in US stumbled on a pornographic magazine and saw this girl sleeping with three men. The page of the magazine was sent to the man who sent it to the lady's family. Of course, that put an end to the marriage proposal. These men are hawks, the type of people that sell the future of young people for their selfish interest. It is up to you to redeem your future by saying firm "NO" to anything vices and any anti-social behaviour that can terminate your destiny, no matter the temporary relief or pleasure it will earn you.

The other class of people we have are those that can be compared with eagles and eaglets, the uncommon birds. These people do not see the way others see because they are visionary. They operate from the level that is not common to either the chicken or the hawk. They know what they want in life and how to get it. They do not see any difficulty in achieving their goals as long as it is possible because they know they can be what they want to be if they put enough efforts into it. As the eagles soar in the air, seeing all opportunities to get what they want either in the water or on the land or on top of the trees, these people can imagine what they want and can see how to get it right on their beds. As strong as lions are, they cannot see as much opportunities as the eagles. Likewise, people that are compared with eagles may not be as powerful or wealthy or well connected like people who can be compared with lions but they see opportunities to excel more than others. They are always preparing themselves to fly higher than other birds because that is what makes them outstanding. The eagles do not go after what the chickens or hawks go after. They are different from those that step over one another to get chicken feeds.

Eagles cannot be caged like chicken. They would die trying to get out. The good news about all these classes of people is that anybody can choose to be what he wants to be. It is not a matter of luck or destiny but a matter of choice.

I use to see people struggling to leave their countries in Africa, looking for green pastures as if the countries they are going are paved with gold. They probably do not realize that a chicken in Africa is a chicken in any part of the world. Going to Europe does not make it an eagle. Be an eagle and stay an eagle wherever you are. If you remain a chicken, you risk falling prey of any of the hawks that fly everywhere, looking for opportunity to devour you or your potentials to be great in life. Do not be a hawk that risks being shot by the hunter (the law). Be an eagle that has nothing to worry about. God has given everybody equal opportunities to soar in the environment he has put us. The Bible says in Isaiah 40: 31, *"But they that wait upon the Lord shall renew their strengths; they shall mount up with wings as eagles; they shall run, and not be weary; and they shall walk, and not faint."*

A CALL FOR IMMEDIATE ACTION

Most of the points in this book are summarized for you to memorize, practice and utilize in the ten guidelines for success given by a very successful man called Marshal Field. He said:

(1) The value of time - don't waste it
(2) The value of perseverance - don't give up.
(3) The pleasure of hard work - don't be lazy.
(4)The dignity of simplicity - don't be complicated
(5) The worth of character - don't be dishonest
(6) The power of kindness - don't be uncaring
(7) The call of duty - don't shun responsibility
(8)The wisdom of economy - don't be a spendthrift
(9) The virtue of patience - don't be impatient
(10)The improvement of skill - don't stop practicing.

I would like to add these four points to make it whole:
(i) The value of human lives - promote peace (ii) The value of Godliness - campaign against vices (iii) The value of Gospel truth - preach it and (iv) The value of eternal value of salvation - do everything to keep it.

Having gone through this course, you can now begin to

take action. It is not enough to learn all the principles of success. You must put them into practice. Do not think of the time you will spend to reach your goal. A thousand mile journey begins with a step. Start the journey from where you are. Read the book over and over again if that will make you fully digest the contents of these lessons. I love people going into action. The best help you can get anywhere in the world is the one you are ready to give yourself.

When you become successful as I desire for you, please, do not forget those coming behind you. Remember that they are counting on you for their own successes in life just as you count on others for your own success.

I do hope the little I have rendered in this book is good enough to help you.

www.ingramcontent.com/pod-product-compliance
Lightning Source LLC
Chambersburg PA
CBHW021339290326
41933CB00038B/987